Altered States

Altered States Contents
The States of

Acknowledgements

The States of California, New Mexico, Wyoming, Montana, Idaho, Mississippi, Florida, Georgia, South Carolina, Illinois, Iowa, Wisconsin, New Jersey, New York, Connecticut, Rhode Island Massachusetts, and Vermont were published in a collaboration collection by Rose Bank Press with poems by Michael Estabrook called *States of Mind.* Some of these poems were in a different form.

As were individual poems State of Connecticut published as The Second Coming by the Chester A Jones National Poetry Competition. This poem received a commendation. The States of Florida, South Carolina and Tennessee were published by Longhouse, The State of New Hampshire by Tin Wreath, The State of Ohio by Impetus, The State of Texas by South Ash Press, The State of Utah by Unknowns, The State of West Virginia was published by Welter, The State of Wyoming by Lucky Star and the State of Vermont by Dog River Review (under another title)
The State of New York by Occasional Review

The Original manuscript of *Altered States* was accepted by Omnation Press as the winner of a book contest but was never published. The current version of the text represents a revision, sometimes with completely different material.

The State of Alabama

All of them good old boys. Evacuating long
neglected back woods land, flattening low mounds
of earth, crushing brittle sticks, ancient skulls,
cracked clay jugs. Quietly crossing sacred lines
distinguishing the living from the dead,
rest beneath tall shade trees shielded
from the high noon sun, eating devil dogs,
corn dogs, sipping Pabst Blue Ribbon cans,
they dream of dry barren acres of dust and bone
among the uprooted stumps of trees, the plantations
burning, field of cotton, turning black.

The State of Alaska

The artist in the north
hears them, voices from
the tundra he wants to
to record. Listening, he wants
to compose suites for wind
instruments, broken strings,
and mixed choirs. In this land
of midnight suns, his dreams
are too fitful to write down,
are too jumbled, overlapping,
rigid, the way layers of ice
and snow are once the deep
freeze is what life is now.
His shallow breathing
nearly freezes at the lips,
sinks down to his blackening
lungs each time he exhales.
What emerges from his mouth
is like steam escaping from
a hand iron, like heat from a
blasted furnace. Falling asleep
is nothing more than another
way to die.

The State of Arizona

In open air markets, fruit seller's
produce is ripe with flames.
All the cherry pits, recumbent eggs,
white fleas, and death watched
beetles are born here, burrowing
within. Their birth breeds colonies
like ants shorn of legs, sprouting wings
that flower as apricots and figs,
trees whose leaves are conical
as cancers, suppurating as wounds.
Alien caterpillars thrive in tent cities,
freak born as beasts, irrational as evolving
geometric forms; look up, the sky is full of them.

The State of Arkansas

Linking arms, they dance on barren
plains, chant Latin verses sotto voce,
invoking insubstantial forms, lighting
seven concentric rings of fire, casting
aside their black ceremonial robes,
kneel down beside broken tree stumps
to better feel the decimated soil,
to draw out long buried hearth stones.
Their conjuring reshapes the storm-swept
village square, reimagines new moon hunters
intent at their work of gutting the catch,
see themselves as specters, long shadows
beside a wasting bonfire. Settling down
in black chalk circles they read entrails
foretell a future that has no sun in it.

The State of California

Flying west, there is nothing down
below, hundreds of miles of waste
where the money crops no longer grow.
We can see them: creatures escaping from
The Fault, moving through the desert,
shedding black slime and muck, their hard
dark skins named like freeways men walk
beside, hitchhiking a mirage, riding a wide
open range into a death valley nights have
nothing inside them but sand hardening
as cement.

The State of Colorado

Inside recessed cliff dwellings overlooking
the mesa tips, overlooking a sloping tree lined
gorge, overlooking white water rapids valley,
overlooking wildlife skirting the shoreline,
scree fall, a scattering of arrowheads, roots,
ancient sundials carved into the rock that
cast long, pointed shadows that tell no time.
Inside the fortress erected here, a study in solitude,
all the empty byways smelling of vegetable rot,
animal carcasses, hanging skins. Withdrawn
ascension ladders lie in a smoking, slow fire
near where condors perch on parapet tips watching
hogan lights die out one by one, withdrawing
all the vital heat source from the sun, committing
the night to an endless barren winter of scattered
freeze-dried bones no fortune teller can read.

The State of Connecticut

They park their four-wheel drive trucks
in a circle, wagon train style, quartz
lanterns turned inward toward the source;
just another ordinary evening in New Haven
waiting inside air-conditioned cabins,
smoking hash pipes, winding up Willie Nelson
tapes, flip top Miller twelve packs iced up
right, brand new silver lensed aviator shades,
boxes of shot gun shells, 20 ought 20's,
midnight blue Yankee caps and pennants,
fresh popped second coming corn; heeding
an inner summons they sit, boxing out the night
with artificial light, armed for the resurrection,
staking their claims for a promised land.

The State of Delaware

Climbing creaking stairs, the cat urine reek,
neglected day care center sand boxes,
strep throat, crying babies behind locked doors
in subdivided rental rooms with cooking stoves,
reeking of hot rancid olive oil, of braised garlic
turning as brown as the air leaking out from
under rag stuffed doors. Inside a room
of one's own, turning down the sheets,
listening to strained, operatic voices filtered
through Bose speakers, plaster walls,
forced arias of long-lost loves and lying
down exhausted with those spectral voices
of other worlds. Deep dreaming unimaginable
sights, dark floating islands of sea grass,
offset by white full moonlit dunes,
whipping sand swept eyes sleep seeing
through rippled molded concrete ceilings,
an invading flock of red wing blackbirds
clotting the white depths of these spectral rooms.

The State of Florida

Swamp gas fires link hanging
cypress trees, natives hear stories
generations old in the wind, hear chanting
voices in still airless nights, hear of corn
whiskey drinkers speak of black magic curses,
of lost tribes worshipping copperhead snakes,
wearing bracelets of alligator teeth, sleeping
near quicksand pits that disappear overnight.
Inland, power boat propellers clog with lumps
of grass, empty boats remain marooned,
overgrown, heavy as swamp rats and rain;
marsh side dwellers point toward the darkened
corner of the pit, directing the park rangers
inside: none may ever pass this way again.

The State of Georgia

Death row begins in a room without
bars, an overturned table, broken
Bud Lite bottles, country western
jukebox music, dimly lighted, not
air conditioned, summer heated smoke,
wooden overhead fan blades, black
puddles of beer and blood where the cracked
skull meets the boot sole tarnished brass
rail. In the stunning silence after the act,
no one dares move. Outside, in the exercise
yard, inmates walk in a single file, chained
one to the other, carrying road working
tool. Twenty years of hard labor rewarded
with a cell, deep breathing slow leaking cyanide
gas, watching the high white clouds tainted
yellow, quickly turning slate gray, then,
totally black.

The State of Hawaii

Cresting the cone, looking down into
the pit: red molten matter, dark layers
of steam and smoke, crematory ash, pulp
rising to the rim. In the guts: pearl divers
breaching the fired waves, trapped,
under the volcano. Inside: black seams,
lava scars. On the coast: palm tree lined
beach fronts, white acres of sand,
tourist trap resort hotels, salt water fishing,
scuba divers feeling the tides, the bending
waves, the rift.

The State of Idaho

Bent, dwarf scrub trees,
the snow lines where nothing
ever grows.
Barren white-faced columns of hard
packed rock, new growth mountains,
porous crescent moon rocks,
tunnels; no sanctuaries here! signs.
Descending, the underbrush thickens,
calcified by cold, transforming
into bundles of ice, sharp hot needles
that electrify night.
What has escaped from the tunnels struggles
to move on down to where all
the deformed creatures reside.

The State of Illinois

Commuter train windows obscure the landscape:
the hidden trees, two-family houses,
double exposed black topped playgrounds,
broken down mirrors of light filtered through
hard layers of mud, rainbow patterns of oil,
the cracked spines of glass.
Tunneling inside: the rushed hours, pressing
fingers stripping the interior, exposing dried
bones, an enclosed terminus of empty box cars,
the disembodied caught, underground, a series
of dark burrows of fetid wind.

The State of Indiana

Night time park side water fountains
misting spray, wild animal noises contained
by thick iron rails, hanging low clouds
of industrial smog. Wooden benches are
illuminated from above: the broken slats,
obscene suggestions painted on stone
supports, overturned trash cans spilling
secrets of lost urban life. On paved pedestrian
paths, endless patterns of broken glass,
discarded bottle caps, torn wine labels,
Gallo Thunderbirds coated by slime and
blood. In the distance: police sirens, fire trucks,
ambulance calls, one after the next
a multitude of stray dogs howling.

The State of Iowa

Birds that never land clog
the sky, spread daunting wings,
touch the tips of trees, blot out
whole fields of crops,
drink rain water from the sky
as it falls, emit rolling thunder
from their tongues as they rest
as a mass inside the thunderhead
clouds, swarming, gathering strength
unleashing black ice, hail stones the color
of their eyes that fall with the rain.

The State of Kansas

Hours after dark, the first ones come,
dipping down into the fields, cutting
through trees, their rotating blades whipping
the tall grass, flat against the earth,
as they land. Klieg lights flood
the open ground, emergency sirens,
two-way radio white noise, loud speakers
broadcasting: able, baker over and out,
looking up, the sky is filled with them.

The State of Kentucky

Summer camps in the still of night,
fireflies tapping cracked glass panes,
swarming moths attending uncovered bulbs.
The screened-in porch is alive with insect life,
covered lawn chairs spread flaking rust,
torn gauze curtains sway, laden with large black
flies. Inner rooms smell of garbage,
stale kegs of beer, broken cases of rum
and straight sour mash. The leaking pipes
spread iron wreathes upon the porcelain double
sinks, treble hooks litter the buckling linoleum
floor; eyeless, severed fish heads stare
straight down into the ruined maze of the camp.

The State of Louisiana

Parading revelers come dressed as pirates,
brigands on shore, exploring the common
market space, afflicted by spirits, the mashed
bourbons and the coke, their wide Halloween
eyes behind ballroom masks, watching a bonfire
of used parts, wrecked cars, then the unchecked
looting, the public burnings on the village greens.
In the harbor, an aptly named, Flying Dutchman
ship, full sails set awaiting the sea. On shore
the looting continues: a conflagration, smoking ruins,
a saxophonist's lament, liturgical jazz.

The State of Maine

Cold reinforces walls cut from granite,
panels of double thick glass
crystallizes, snow buries the dwarfed
heads of trees, smoke freezes at the source
adding a skin of stone harder than the ice
packed against the northern walls.
Snowbound for the duration, feeling
the pressure of layered snow pressing in
through dry walls, the insulated ceiling panels,
layers of rugs coating the floors,
then the breaking open pipes, the sealing off
of last registers of heat; outside, the frozen
earth cracks open.

The State of Maryland

Scavenger birds pick through low tide
ruins: the beached crabs baking in the sun,
the cracked mussel shells and round moss
covered stones, the broken sticks half buried
by sand. Black flies swarm above the receding
shoreline, attracted by the scent, the standing
fetid water changing chemical colors,
overcoating covers of oil, ethylene rainbows.
Posted signs forbid smoking, lighting fires,
all trespassing is a confinable offense.
From the collapsing, soiled, last wasted ridge
dunes the ocean is a burnt offering to
a scorched earth sun.

The State of Massachusetts

Old New Bedford whalers live by
shorelines scattered with bones.
They lift their eyes from land to
read by flaming pools of cetacean oil,
tread a widow's walk, whistling all
hands on deck tunes, feel the warping
boards creak, ascend winding metal stairs
down into the hold, confident all four sails
are furled full. In the crow's nest, preparing
for pursuit, night watches spot the spume;
down there, on the beach, leviathans
are leaping from their bones, missing the sea.

The State of Michigan

Smog layers the lake, fog horns
cut the dark into parcels, blocks
of impenetrable stone, cargo ships
are totally lost within, blind and rigid
aiming useless lights toward masses
of land listening for warning buoy
bells, tracing fingers over navigational
charts, sounding the depths inside
individual cabin cells, feeling
the shifting rocks, the dull throbbing
engines urging the infernal machine on,
deeper into the night.

The State of Minnesota

Free floating the night currents,
fishing lines cut the broken mirror
of moons lighting the wind-swept lake.
Starting power motors, interrupts
the fluid passages of migratory birds
touching down from the sky along side
matted islands of grass. Mid-lake casting
artificial lures into the wind, treble hooked live
bait catches the taut lips of the shrunken
heads of drowned sailors, rising, resurrected,
resurfacing an inland sea with flesh.

The State of Mississippi

Driven to the forest, hunters examine
rude paths, charting forward progress
by the motion of the sun overhead.
Hunting bear requires patient days,
night flasks of hard whiskey, beef jerky,
hard boiled eggs by the fireside.
Night watching reveals full moon shadows
Breaking the heads of clustered trees,
igniting the senseless eyes of the beast,
drawn toward light. The scent of man
is stronger than either pain or fear,
encourages Bear to rise onto his hind legs,
to stealth move slowly downstream
toward the kill.

The State of Missouri

They are crusaders for Christ whose faith
has been amplified by days and nights spent
coddling serpents, thin black asps, striped
rattlers, puff adders, copperheads and
copper backs. A venomous bite brings death
in minutes or in hours, to mere mortals who
have not managed the touching and handling
of snakes, nor mastered the grammar
of glossolalia and tongues of others.
Their recorded voices are unrecognizable,
as their own, and transcripts of their
speaking could be a movie exorcist would
run from clutching burning bibles imbued
with the word of the word of the horned one
vocalized. Still, they preach, every day,
behind backyard pulpits or in revival tents,
in fundamental churches and in backwoods
storefronts, proclaiming the handling must
go on, tongues respected, especially the ones
that warn of sinners in the hands of God,
of the ones holding snakes, sayeth the Lord,
"Danger Is Only One Letter Removed From Anger."

The State of Montana

Dust collects on the back bar bottles.
No one ever sees the hand gliding
through the tarnished mirror, touching
cash register keys, polishing shot glasses,
emptying ash trays from the bar.
All day drinking in the heat requires
Watching fat honeyed bees, unfiltered cigarette
ends turning cremation gray, listening
as the juke box plays old country western
love/death/hate songs, watching as the slate
gray sky turns storm cloud black, feeling
the heat lightning extending shell glasses,
electrifying neural veins, short circuiting
terminally blood shot eyes.

The State of Nebraska

They sit in wheel chairs, five stories
of them, dying, these petrified people
confined by apartment rooms, remaindered
human beings overlooking the cultivated land,
waiting, unable to move old age wasted arms,
their bent, arthritic hands clutching vinyl bags.
Sitting, they are little more than bed sore
infested thighs, useless, crippled feet inside
designer brand running shoes, effigies behind sliding
glass doors, hermetically attached to tall cylinders
of oxygen, white breathing masks. Always nearly
asleep even while awake, afflicted, their
unplugged hearing aids, metal hair curling rods,
stimulants for the heart and the mind. On the Plains
heat blisters the failing fields.

The State of Nevada

Suns never set inside houses without windows,
self-contained plush carpeted halls,
the gambling tables, roulette wheels,
trays of free drinks circulate all twenty-four
hours, bright overhead fixtures eternally
extend daylight savings time, air conditioning
units circulate the smoke. Life has no meaning
beyond these four sealed walls, watchers are
isolated behind one way glass mirrors
in booths above the gaming tables scanning
the floor, monitoring the action, reducing
laws of chance, fixing the gross statements
of profit and loss, never resting, their eyes
turned inward. Sleep only comes near the end
of the game.

The State of New Hampshire

Inside, the disturbed children draw
horror masks with colored chalks,
lie down for days in corners under chairs
refusing to move, watch birds fly inside,
crossing their eyes, making them laugh
so hard nothing can stop the tears, the crying
out, their crawling in rows on all fours
in the night, silent as cats in the hallway.

The State of New Jersey

Sloping strings of carnival lights
hang low over the boardwalk,
smart talking barkers sell tickets,
fast foods, side door freak shows,
endless rides on motion sickness machines.
Riders turn upside down, pinned
flat against the spinning metal wheel,
unable to move, rigid arms clutching
support rails, wide bulging, white only
eyes, forced bubbles of sweat and blood,
compressed air, straining lungs about
to burst.

The State of New Mexico

Navaho country. No one outside the tribe
completely understands the modern ways
of warriors buried standing up on a barren
plain, shooting dust devils with 20
ought 20's, drinking red eye express train
whiskey, staring downwind into the desert.
Their ancestors owned the afterworld,
heavily armed for every hunt, stood tall
among herds cloaked in robes of buffalo and elk,
prepared for what must be: endless trails
inside, festering seams of night, the sky bending
where it meets the earth. In the red slit before
night the last warriors dance

The State of New York

Victory gardens sacked by hordes of rats,
rabid grey squirrels, moonlit nights,
they can be heard invading the garbage,
scavenging the frozen yards of ruts,
eating through the meshed wire screens,
butting heads pressed against a double
thickness of basement glass. Looking up,
behind stone cellular walls, through
the hanging spider webs, the crystallized
window panes deformed by scratching,
are the red ferret eyes, staring, glowing the dark.

The State of North Carolina

Cape Fear is the winter, white frozen
lumps of sand, balls of snow, dried weeds
blown seaward, night stopping broken waves,
twisted cross currents, full moon lit
beach rock casting dark cutting shadows
underwater. Ice clings to stone, rusting
iron, steel reinforced concrete bases
of stark storm turrets, lighthouses
without windows, sealed doors, dominate
the receding beachfront hardened by cold,
overlooking amorphous creatures of the night
moving steadily inland. Red distress lights
in the Bay beckon, distract long boats off shore.

The State of North Dakota

Rowing out into the night
of the Northern sun, leaving bodies
of land without life, decrepit shacks
sinking into marsh, clumps of dry
yellowed reeds, clusters of islands,
wharf moorings sinking into the lake,
broken docks without boats, dried black
fishing nets casting long webbed shadows
on the dead, still waters.

The State of Ohio

Old women comb their unwashed hair
with black plastic forks, lie down
to dream on park benches where they
speak to the sun. Their words are black birds
leaping out between clouds, demanding
a new kind of rain, asking for paper bags
of air to escape sleep in. Their dreaming
compresses silence to a ring of worms,
redefining textured concepts of skin and
bone. After dark, heads between their knees,
the old women cough up their lives onto
Sunday Supplement pages old men collect
in the morning.

The State of Oklahoma

Riding shotgun, the enormous old woman
peels bruised bananas, wears filthy
blue raincoats, torn house dresses,
her bewigged hair contained by tie-dyed
bandanas. She hails rushing VW vans,
bearing old men wearing string pull ties,
silk cravats, maroon knit ties, red
polyester pants, smoking El Ropo cigars,
summoning hunched backed men
who drag their burlap sacks through
the gutter dust, collect discarded butts,
sandwich rinds, dandelion stems.
These days they run in packs along major
highways, riverside roads, their white
stuttering lips carrying a communal plague
of high fevered dreams.

The State of Oregon

Watching for fire extends the tree line
beyond the coast, empties the artificial
seeded clouds of moisture, blackens animal
tongues testing humps of grass for vital
signs of water. Overturned rocks expose
insect colonies, centuries of dry rot,
releases a small universe of dormant suns
from beneath black lumps of burying soil,
frees the trapped spirits of the night
who come bearing the secret of fire on their lips.

The State of Pennsylvania

Steel ribbed cages, white faced concrete
factories, ribbed windows punched out,
asbestos wrapped piping bridging one way
streets into deserted, Mechanicville yards.
Rusted barbed wire fencing, black stencil
spray painted signs directs traffic south,
under reinforced walkway arches deeper
into the idle machine. Welcome to Carnegie:
empty lots, piles of asphalt and of brick,
coal dust and rotten eggs, black towers
of smoke, fracking smog, invisible death.

The State of Rhode Island

Beach fires leave a thin coat
of ash, blackened drift wood,
scorched stones, discarded
cooking sticks coated with sugar
and sand, bent cans and Rolling Rock
bottles. Sweeping inland, touching
down in funnels, cones of cyclonic
air give off light, project summer
storms that break down the sky
a layer at a time.

The State of South Carolina

Trash collectors drag old stoves
from the backs of unpainted open trunks
in the dead of night, hand crank manual
clothes drying machines, inspect cast iron
double sinks in a driving rain,
oil cordless industrial fans. Their yards are
filled with Hot Point refrigerators, spare
car parts, rusting engine blocks, plastic
clothes lines, drying overalls, wet greased
denim work shirts. Nothing that ever worked
is thrown away. Early mornings, before dawn,
they are the shadows moving clothes trees,
high backed wicker chairs, Grandfather clocks,
store front wooden cigar Indians.
Inside, behind locked doors, they are the dark eyes
behind drawn shades sharpening pocket knives,
butchering the livestock. Later that evening,
outside, they stand, transfixed, shouting out
at the moon.

The State of South Dakota

Sacred lands shaped in deformed humps
like those beasts the Sioux gods hunted.
Chasing they went, spreading textured
lights through weird pointed gullies,
worn rock formations, and lean striated towers,
inexplicably left barren, cut dry, a lunar caustic
are the bad lands for the pale men carrying
spears for the killers of Mammoth,
those woolly creatures that grazed the flat grass
on polished plains. Escape is futile, downwind
from the hunting parties, they who rattle their
futile sacred, necklace teeth, shaking the blessed
dried husks of corn, climbing the depths
of a calcified lake swimming the rock.

The State of Tennessee

Whole towns and villages remain
intact underwater in the valley
after the man-made flood. Dams
watercolor the countryside variations
of green, hydroelectric power generates
the city lights while, in the valley, those
who refuse to leave wave their arms,
resisting an antediluvian world,
shouting down the torrents as they come,
ripping down storm doors and windows,
flooding root cellars, smashing hurricane
lamps, overwhelming the streets, furiously
pumping all the way South.

The State of Texas

Zippered seams connect squares of
artificial grass, contained by a
geodesic dome. Visiting outfielders
look up into a supporting web of I-beams
attempting to locate a batted ball,
while outside, the desert sand is alive
with rolling, burning brush.
Inside, the electric scoreboard short
circuits, blacks out in mid-inning,
stranding runners between bases;
the umpires caught looking up,
disbelieving, unaware of the progressing
play, light towers emanating the dark.
Climate control thermostats can no longer be
adjusted; heat rises from the turf
in layers with the smoke.

The State of Utah

All night the desert draws the heat
from above and turns it into cold
hours of sand pressed into glass containers
of sound. Reptiles are moving their hard-shell
backs beneath unturned polished stones,
afraid of moon-shadows cast upon dark
plains where a staged choral group sing
measured quarter notes that stick on
the tips of alternate tongues, pinned to
the source by needles of an unavoidable
heat that rises from within.

The State of Vermont

Unable to avoid sleeping in the heat,
old couples sit in Bentwood rocking
chairs, heads slumping against
sunken chests, wide screen color television
sets cycle prime time channels, remote
controlled reading lamps switch on and off,
intake window fans suck in all forms
of insect life, coating the opposite
faded flower papered walls with dark,
sticky clots. Shorted circuits overload,
ozone gases burn, blaring overhead first alert
alarms. The stunned sleepers awake.
Swarms of gypsy moths attack their wide,
open eyes.

The State of Virginia

Tunnel traffic backs up for miles
behind a four-car wreck, overheating
engines idle, steam fogs shatterproof
windshield glass, bleeds soot covered walls.
A multitude of car horns echo down
chambered halls, gathering force,
an almost living thing then fenders touch,
gears engage, others are urged onward,
chain reactions start puddles of spilled
gas, engine exhaust fumes fill the close
air beneath the Bay, drivers sit, foreheads
pressed against padded steering wheels
waiting for what happens next.

The State of Washington

Summer green seeded lawns, wild climbing
vines, ivy chokes the southern walls,
sunflowers lean against a slanting second
story roof, snow peas climb the cyclone
fence. Northern lights swirl in cold harbors
inset far below, the incessant storm clouds
darker than the heat waves, illusions of
light break down the barriers of acid rain,
free falling layers of death. Each new
downpour is heavier than the last.

The State of West Virginia

Hard, jagged shafts, open black veins
of rock. Underground, hard hats contain
individual lights, become cutting fogs
of dust, expose the seam, third shifts
buried in basement walls staring down
the long angular tomb. Endless coal car
processions traverse the rusting rails,
scraping wheels emit sparks, harsh noises
the miners are deaf to. Digging further down,
becomes a suspended state of animation,
of shadows moving where there is no light.

The State of Wisconsin

Death beds remain unchanged,
disheveled, soiled covers hang down,
protective metal railings frozen in
place, frames irreparably bent,
dozens of rows of them left at odd angles,
in no longer safe rooms.
In the corridors, emergency bedding strapped
to operating tables, piles of linen stacked wall
to wall, used gowns and gloves discarded,
soiled and reeking, disinfected no more.
Everywhere inside, a clinging stench of spilled
fluids, denatured alcohol, body waste, incipient
as death. Everywhere inside, the high-rise hospital
walls, elevator cars stuck where they stopped
in between floors.

The State of Wyoming

Sharp flint arrowheads point up
toward the sky. Beside the interstate:
miles of broken glass, empty wine bottles
cans, anything liquor can be contained in,
discarded. Where the braves once walked
with bare feet into the center of the universe
is a Taco stand, blacktopped parking
lots, drive-in theaters that show X-Rated
movies all night long. Downwind,
in summer, everything smells of
deep fried fat, dead animal skins,
sacrificial fires that summon
lost ancestral spirit ghosts back
to these now forbidding, arid lands.